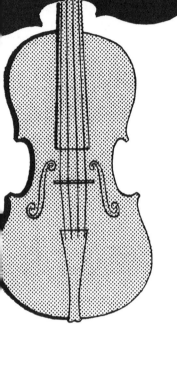

OLIN MASTERS'
Duet Repertoire

COMPILED, ARRANGED AND EDITED

by **HARVEY S. WHISTLER**

and **HERMAN A. HUMMEL**

T0071575

CONTENTS...

		Page
ADAGIO ÉLÉGIAQUE	Ries	18
ALLEGRO DE CONCERT	Gebauer	6
ALLEGRO from the FIRST CANONIC SONATA	Telemann	28
ALLEGRO from the SONATA IN A	Corelli	14
ANDANTE from the DUO SONATA IN G	Tartini	48
AUBADE	De Beriot	33
CANZONETTA	Böhm	42
CONCERTO GROSSO IN D MINOR	Vivaldi	52
CONCERTSTÜCK	Kalliwoda	8
DIVERTIMENTO IN D	Sitt	12
DUDZIARZ (The Country Fiddler)	Wieniawski	25
DUETTINO IN F	Dancla	5
DUO BRILLANTÉ	Rode	26
DUO CÉLÈBRE	Pleyel	2
DUO CONCERTANTE	Viotti	16
DUO DE SALON	Alard	20
DUO DRAMATIQUE	Jansa	41
DUO PERPETUO	Fiorillo	23
DUO POPULAIRE	Mazas	46
DUO SYMPHONIQUE	Campagnoli	10
FANTAISIE BRILLANTE (Duo de Concours)	Leonard	50
FINALE from the SIXTH CANONIC SONATA	Telemann	38
FOLIES D' ESPAGNE (Theme and Variations)	Corelli	44
LA CHASSE	Hoffmeister	27
LA MÉLANCOLIE	Prume	4
MEDITATION from the MILITARY CONCERTO	Bazzini	34
MENUET from the CONCERT-SONATE	Veracini-David	37
MINUETTO from the SUITE ROMANTIQUE	Vieuxtemps	43
MORCEAU LYRIQUE	Dancla	30
MUSETTE from the Second Classical Suite	Leclair-David	24
NOTTURNO-PASTORALE	Molique	19
PIÈCE DE CONCERT	Dancla	31
RONDO-ALLEGRO from the Grand Duo in E♭	Spohr	40
RONDO ELÉGANTE	Kreutzer	22
SALON-DUETT	Hohmann	35
SCHERZO-CAPRICE	Gebauer	13
SOUVENIR POETIQUE	Dancla	36
THEME AND VARIATION on the Air "Barucaba"	Paganini	56
VARIATIONS on the AIR "MONTEGNARD"	De Beriot	32

Rubank®

HAL•LEONARD®
CORPORATION
7777 W. BLUEMOUND RD. P.O. BOX 13819 MILWAUKEE, WI 53213

Duo Célèbre

PLEYEL

2

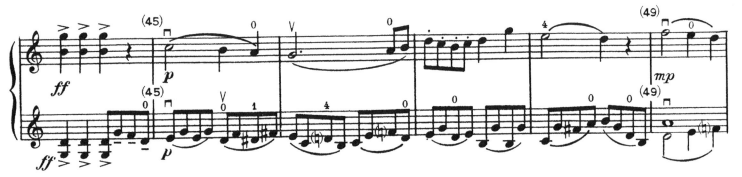

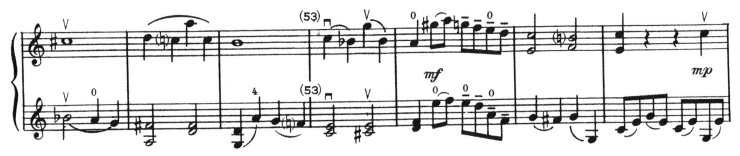

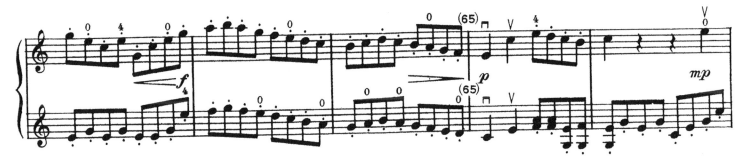

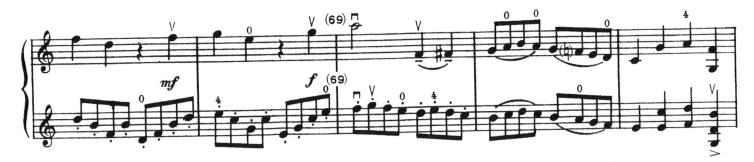

*La Mélancolie

PRUME

Andante sentimentale

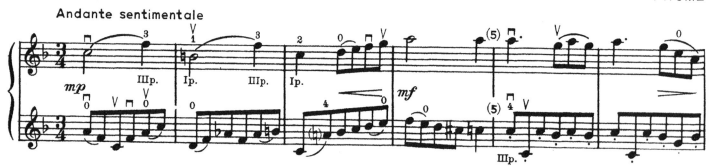

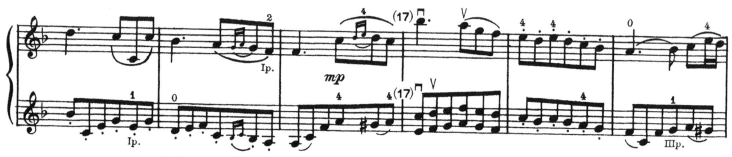

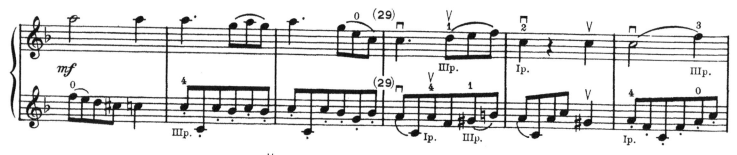

* The most popular violin duet of the 19th Century, *La Mélancolie* brought world-wide fame to its composer.

Duettino in F

DANCLA

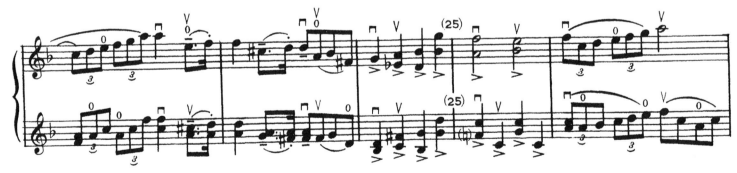

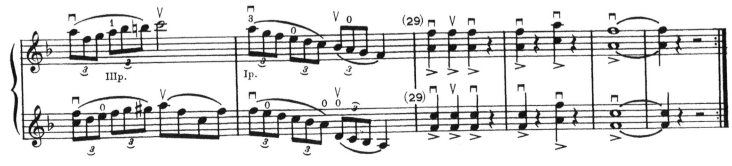

Allegro de Concert

GEBAUER

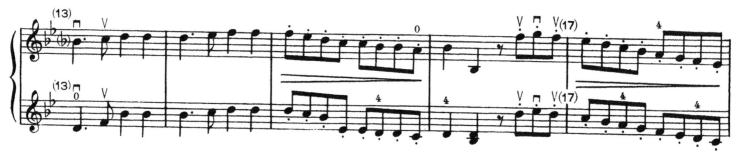

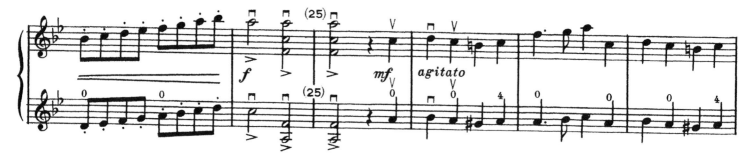

6

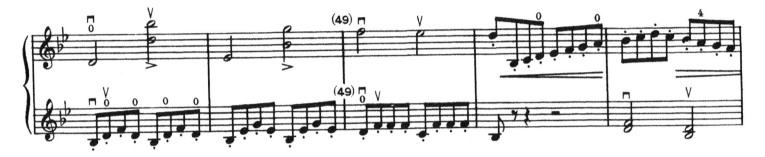

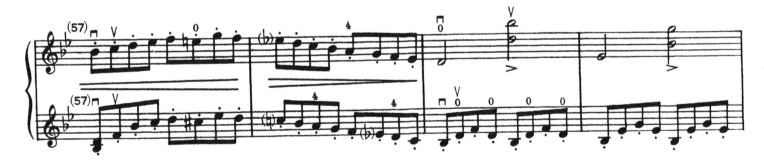

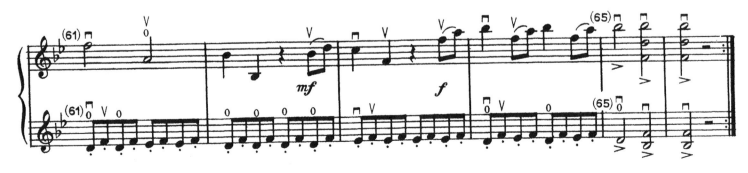

Concertstück

KALLIWODA

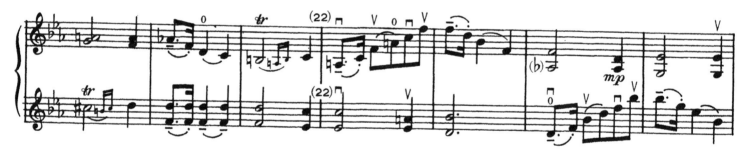

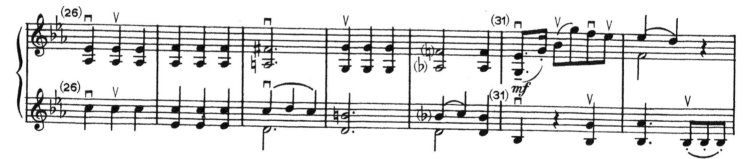

Duo Symphonique

CAMPAGNOLI

Allegro ben moderato

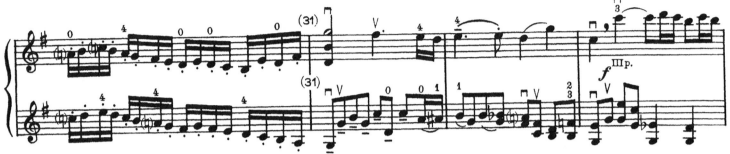

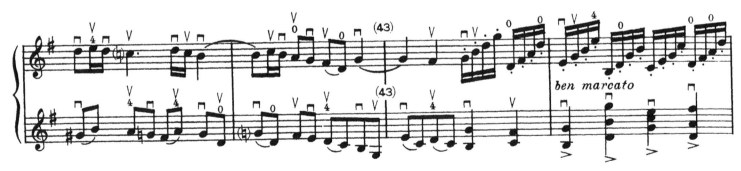

Divertimento in D

SITT

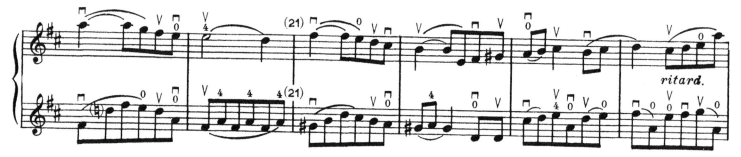

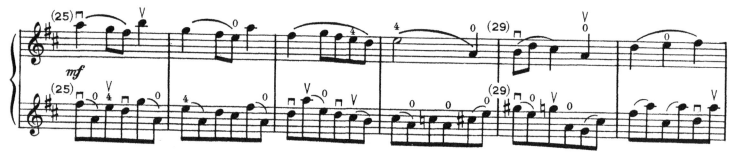

Scherzo-Caprice

GEBAUER

Allegro from the Sonata in A

CORELLI

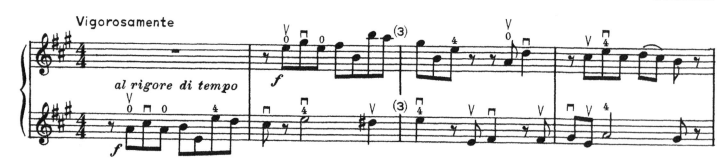

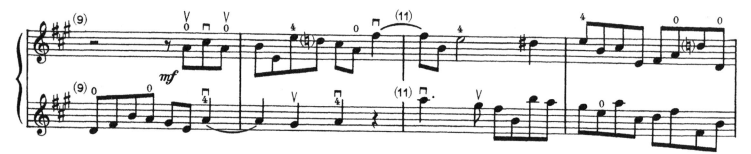

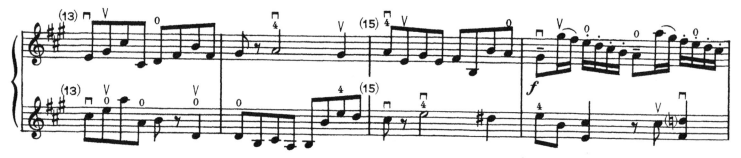

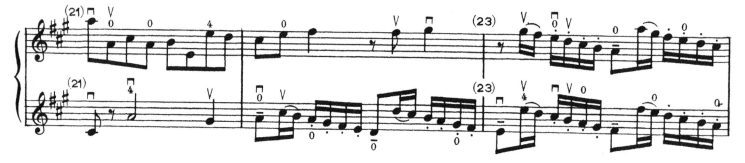

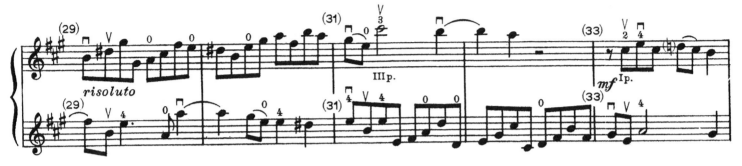

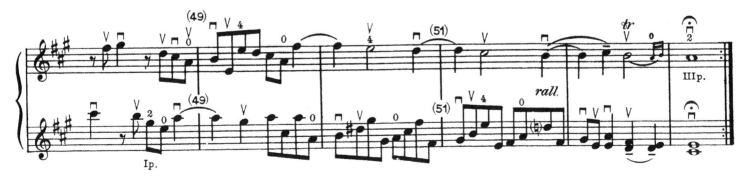

Duo Concertante

VIOTTI

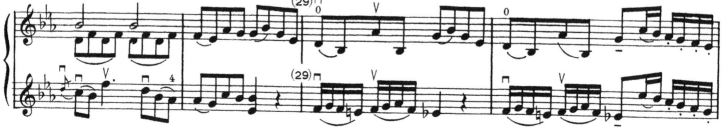

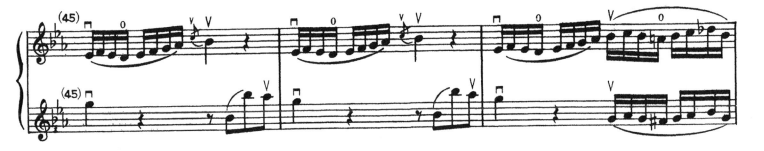

Adagio Élégiaque

RIES

Con affetto

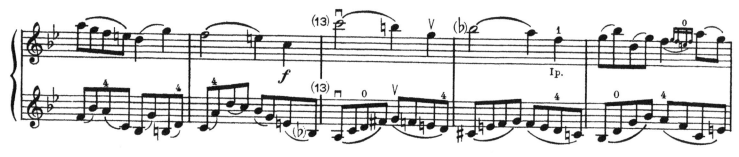

Notturno-Pastorale

MOLIQUE

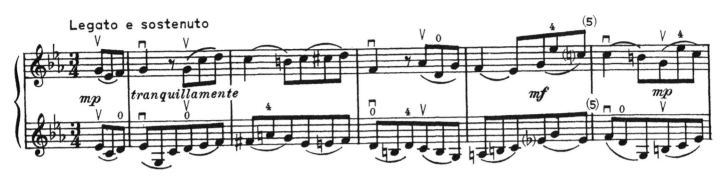

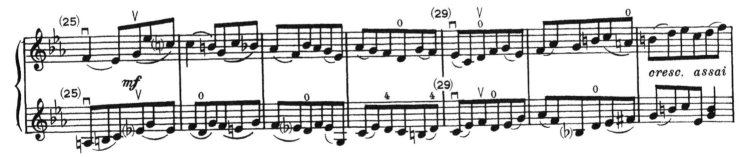

Duo de Salon

ALARD

Amabile

(Remain in fourth position throughout.)

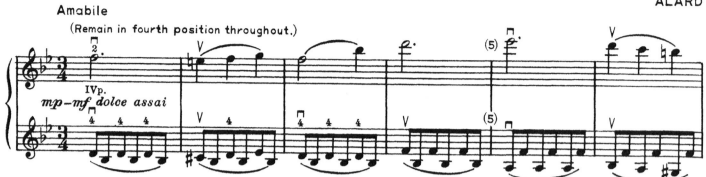

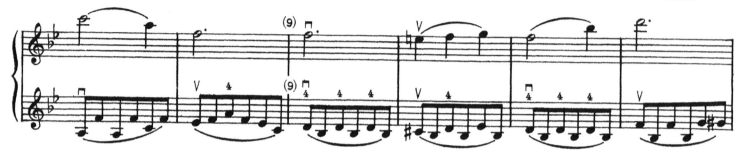

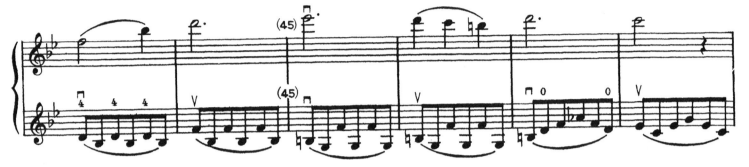

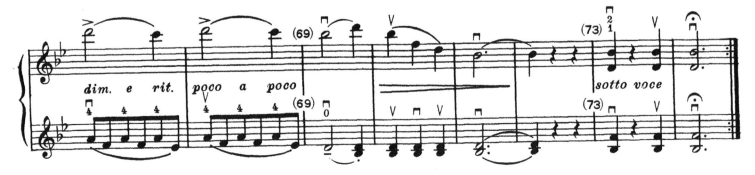

Rondo Elégante

KREUTZER

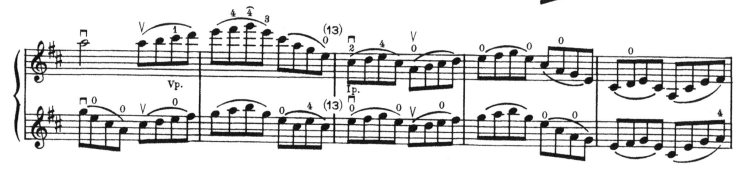

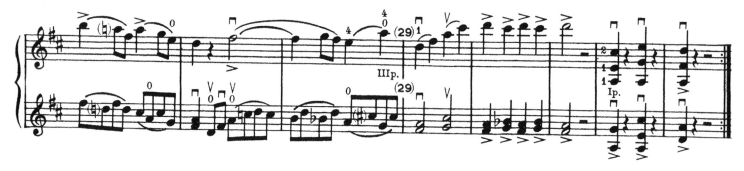

Duo Perpetuo

FIORILLO

Vivace ma non troppo

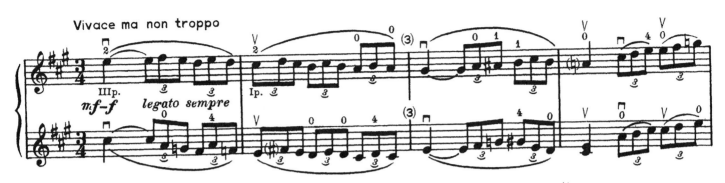

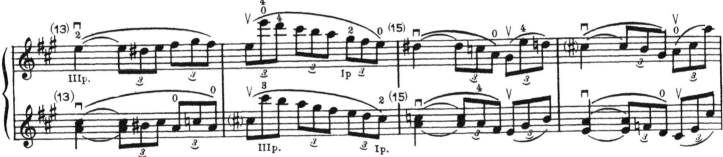

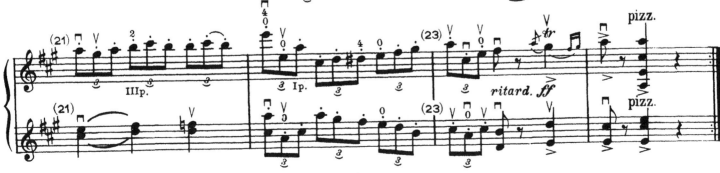

Musette
from the Second Classical Suite

LECLAIR - DAVID

Allegretto e elegante

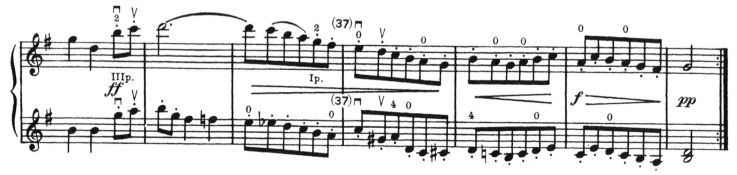

Dudziarz
(The Country Fiddler)

WIENIAWSKI

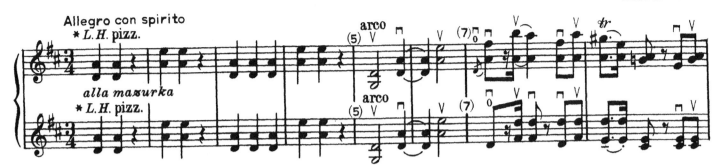

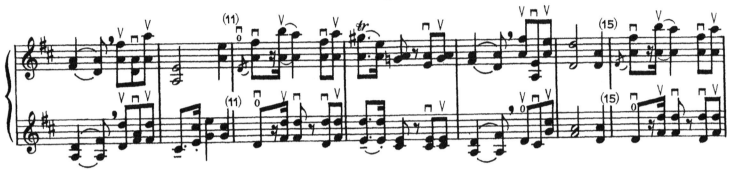

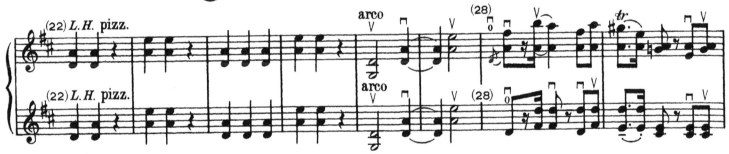

* L.H. pizz. = Left Hand pizzicato.

Duo Brillanté

RODE

La Chasse

HOFFMEISTER

Allegro from the First Canonic Sonata

TELEMANN

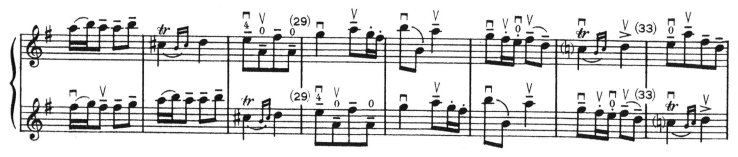

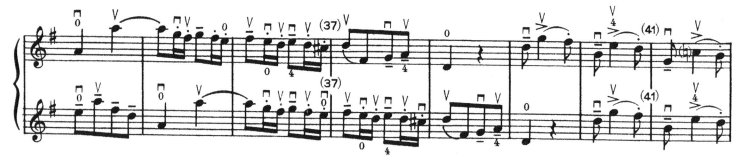

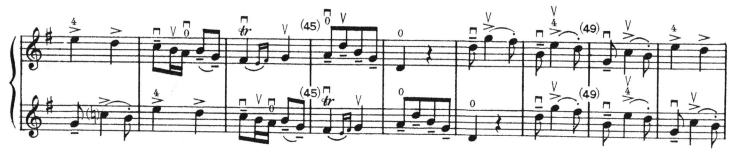

Morceau Lyrique

DANCLA

Pièce de Concert

DANCLA

Variations on the Air "Montegnard"

DE BERIOT

Aubade

DE BERIOT

Andante sostenuto

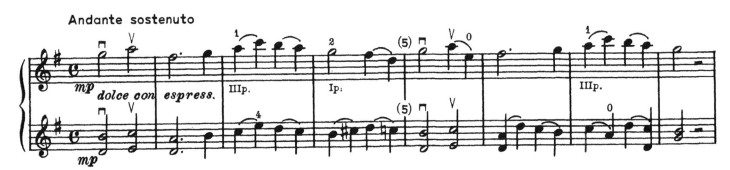

Meditation from the Military Concerto

BAZZINI

Salon-Duett

HOHMANN

Souvenir Poetique

DANCLA

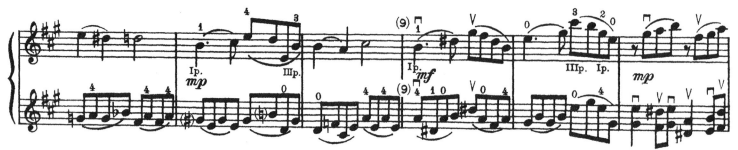

*   2nd finger, IIIp., must touch string lightly for harmonic an octave higher than note fingered.
** 1st finger, IIIp., must touch string lightly for harmonic an octave and fifth higher than note fingered.

Menuet from the Concert-Sonate

VERACINI–DAVID

Finale from the Sixth Canonic Sonata

TELEMANN

Allegramente

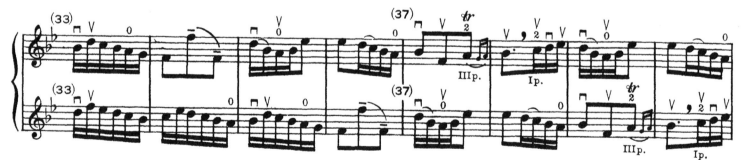

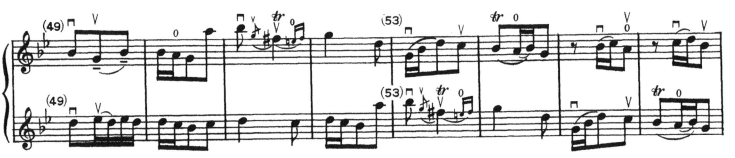

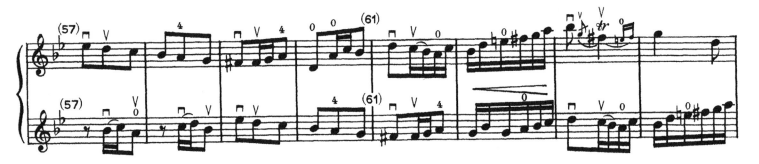

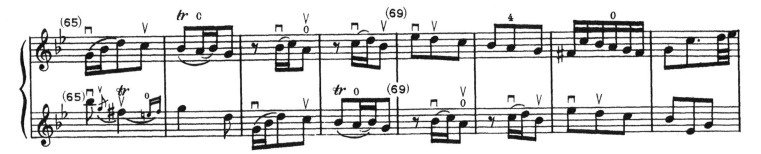

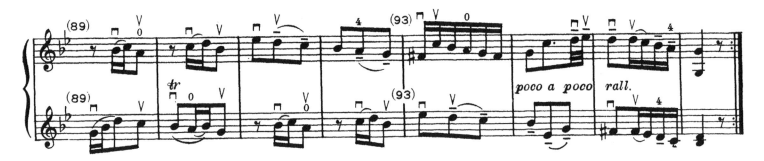

Rondo-Allegro

from the Grand Duo in E♭

SPOHR

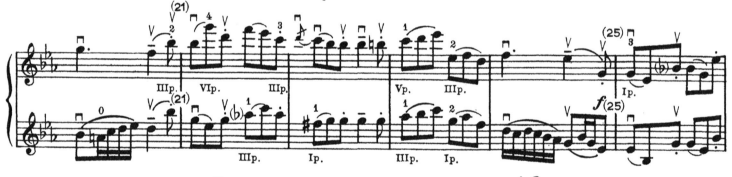

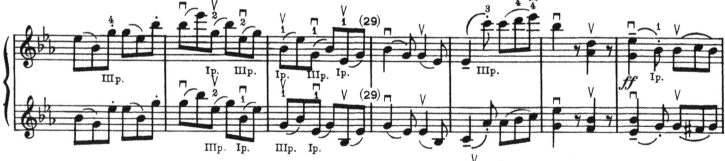

Duo Dramatique

JANSA

Canzonetta

BÖHM

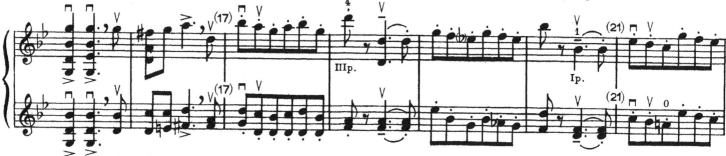

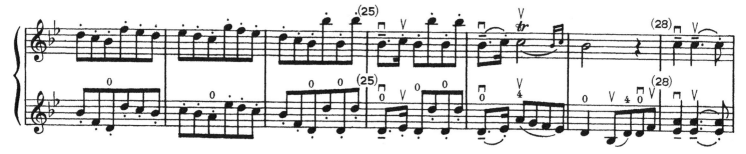

Minuetto from the Suite Romantique

(A Madame La Princesse de Caraman-Chimay)

VIEUXTEMPS

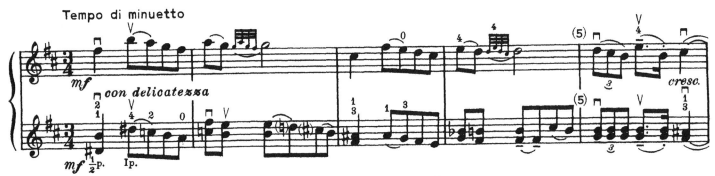

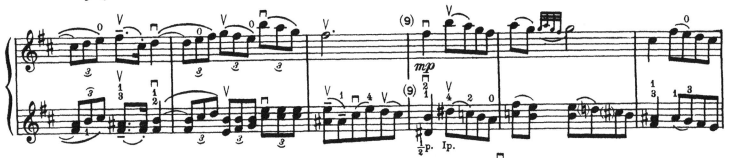

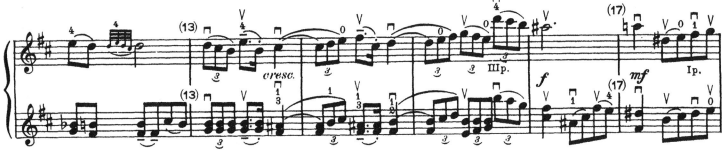

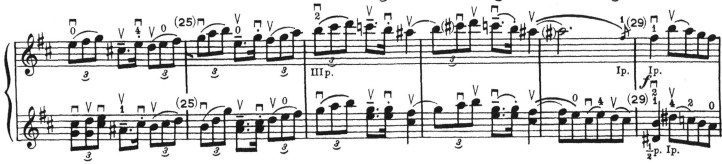

Folies d' Espagne
(Theme and Variations)

CORELLI

Adagio e cantabile

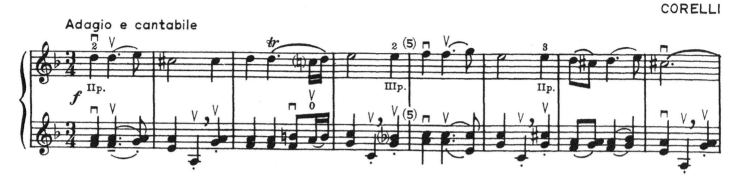

Allegro ma non troppo

VAR. I

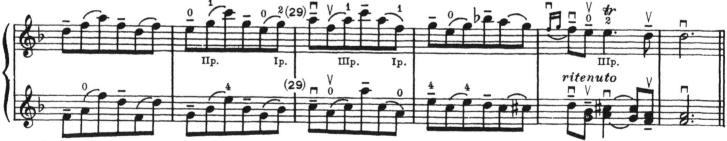

Allegro brillante

VAR. II

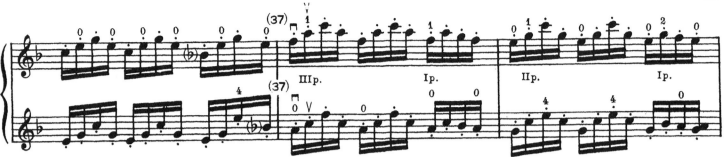

Allegramente e legato

VAR. III

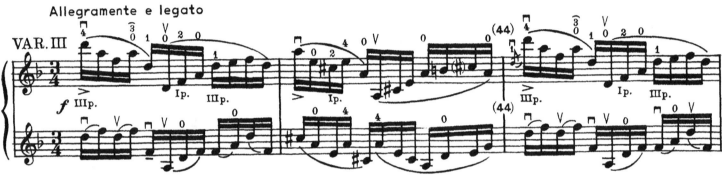

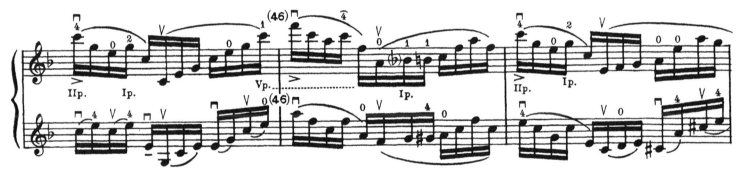

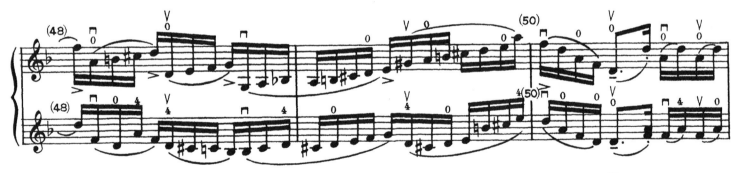

* The open E string should be played while E (2nd finger, IIIp.) is trilled with F (3rd finger, IIIp.).

Duo Populaire

MAZAS

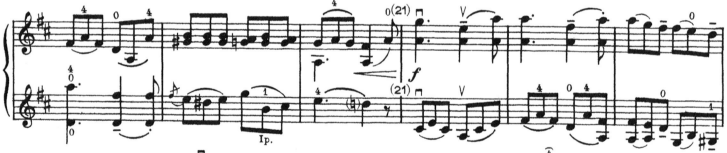

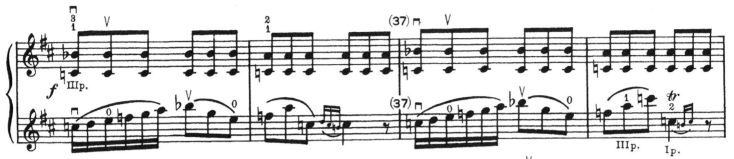

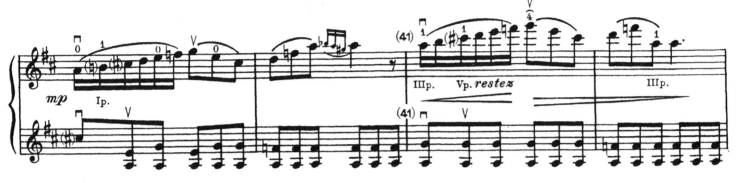

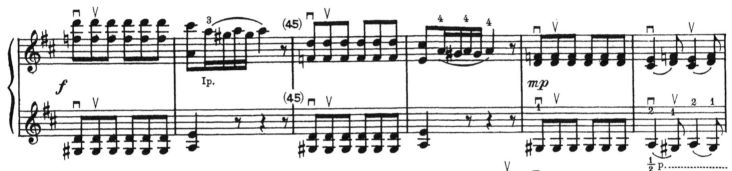

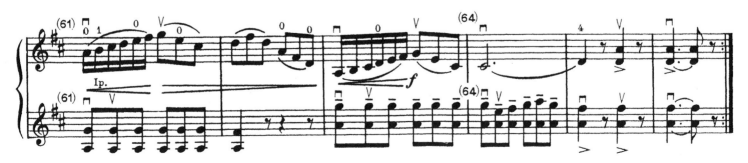

Andante from the Duo Sonata in G

TARTINI

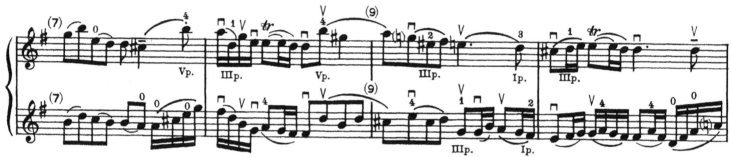

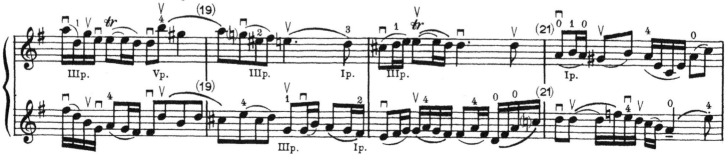

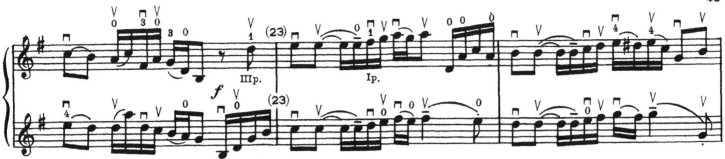

Fantaisie Brillante
(Duo de Concours)

LEONARD

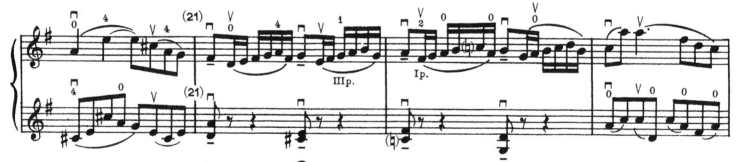

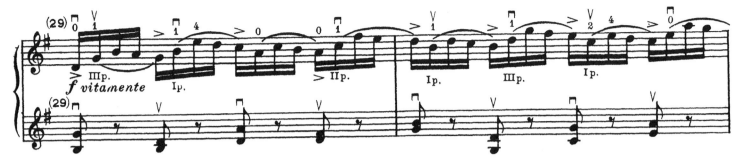

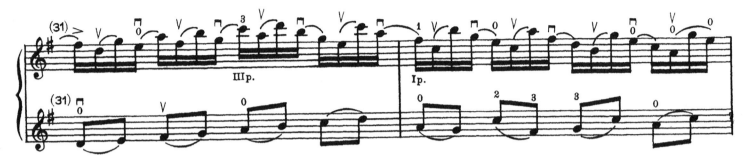

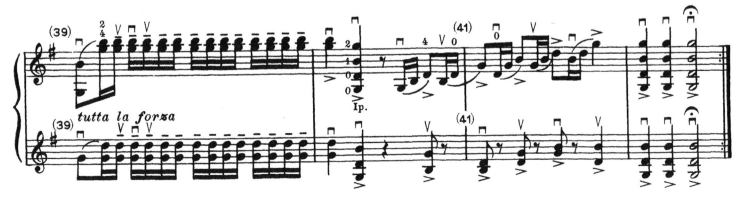

Concerto Grosso in D Minor

VIVALDI

Molto adagio

Allegro

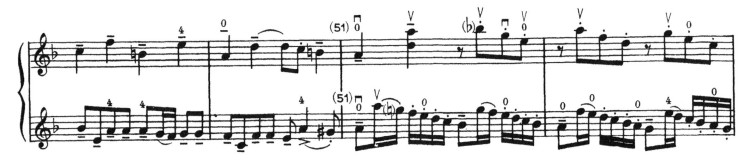

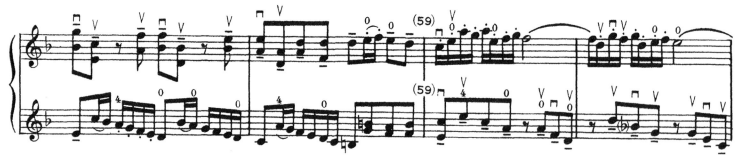

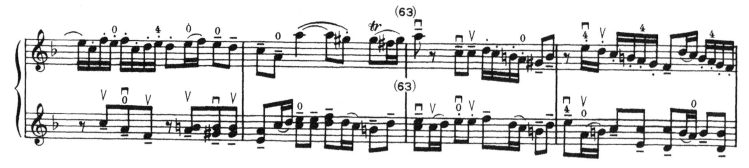

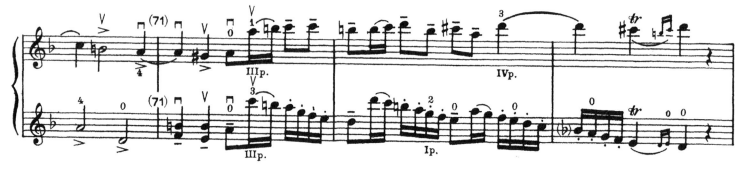

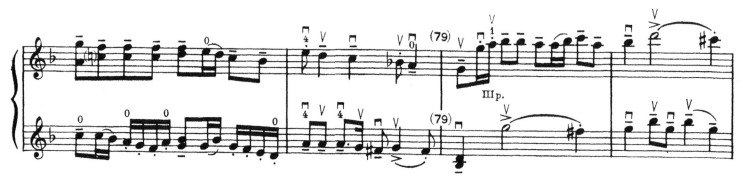

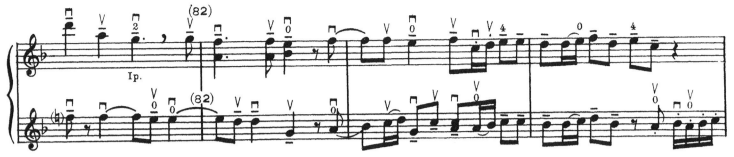

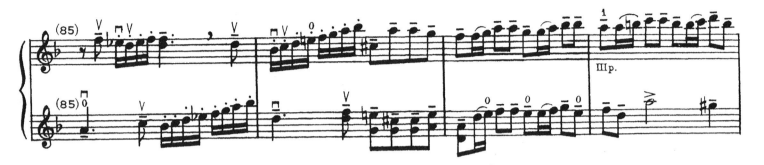

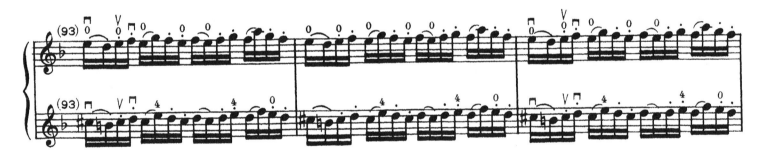

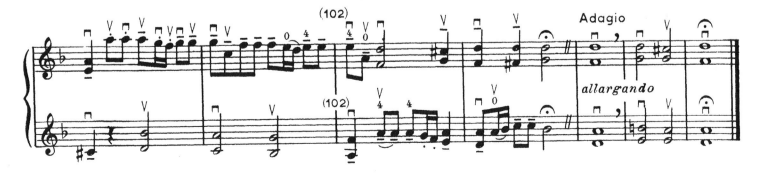

Theme and Variation
on the Air "Barucaba"

PAGANINI

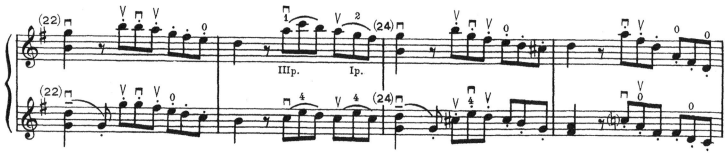